THE YELLOW SUITCASE

Poems

Djelloul Marbrook

FIRST EDITION, November 2025
Library of Congress Control Number: *pending*
ISBN 978-1-965784-24-2 HARDBACK
ISBN 978-1-965784-23-5 PAPERBACK
Printed in the United States of America, Canada, Australia,
Saudi Arabia, Japan, India, Brazil, and the European Union

Graphic Design & Book Typography by Kurt Lovelace.
Cover artwork by Pierian Springs Press Staff
Cover type *Bauhaus Dessau* **Alfarn** by Céline Hurka,
Elia Preuss, Flavia Zimbardi,
Hidetaka Yamasaki, and Luca Pellegrini.
Author name, blurbs, footers in **Jenson** by Robert Slimbach.
Back cover description in **Gill Sans Nova**.
Titles and body text set in **Baskerville**.
Flourishes set in Emigre Foundry **Dalliance** by Frank Heine.
Emigre Foundry **ZeitGuys** by Bob Aufuldish, Eric Donelan.
Typefaces licensed Adobe, Linotype, Emigre, & URW GmbH.

PierianSpringsPress.Com
PIERIAN SPRINGS PRESS, INC
30 N GOULD ST, STE 25398
SHERIDAN, WYOMING 82801-6317

Eternity is the instant that suffices to consume all time.

—Paul Valery

I remember I used to half believe and wholly play
with fairies when I was a child. What heaven can be
more real than to retain the spirit-world of childhood,
tempered and balanced by knowledge and common-sense

—Beatrix Potter, The Complete Tales

Children don't belong to their parents, and they are
only apparently produced by them.

—Carl Jung

 CONTENTS

INTRODUCTION BY KURT LOVELACE

AWASH

TIDES

TIDEWRACK

 ABOUT THE AUTHOR | 100

 PUBLICATIONS | 103

Poetry is the common speech of daemons.
We eavesdrop at our peril.
Changelings are those who overhear.
Never say next episode to daemons,
it's the only capital offense.
Their words are not meant to be graven,
they don't survive the page,
they don't know how to rest;
they're the very search function,
as remorseless as light.

—Djelloul Marbrook

INTRODUCTION
KURT LOVELACE

I did not personally know Djelloul Marbrook. I never heard his voice across a café table, never watched him search for a word in mid-sentence. What I know of him, I know from these poems, and from the fact of his death, November 23rd of 2024.

Initially, I gladly took this project on to help Marc Vincenz of MadHat Press, knowing Marc has a perpetual two year plus backlog of books to get out. Perhaps there felt an urgency at the time, with Marbrook being ill, to rush this work into print. But I myself ended up spending a full year to get this book out, only now, in November of 2025. One must live with a writer's words to truly know them.

This book comes to us as what Marbrook himself might have called "a briefing", a last, concentrated report from a mind that had been paying attention, for a very long time.

THE SUITCASE AS WOUND, RELIQUARY, LAUNCHPAD

The title poem, "The yellow suitcase," tells you at once that this isn't going to be a tidy memoir in verse. The suitcase is cardboard, striped red, black, and green, and the speaker has come "to the shores of Great South Bay" with it in hand, intending to die in a rotting barn "like an equation on a blackboard / awaiting erasure."

That's a harsh, funny, and frightening image all at once, typical Marbrook. He's always doing at least three things at the same time. The yellow suitcase is trauma, certainly: "defiled unbelongings" he's reluctant to unpack. It's also a portable archive of selves, half-caste, bastard, tidewrack, dragged through decades of damage. And it is, unexpectedly, a kind of holy object: a valise of memory that, once set down and opened, releases not just hurt but a flock of salvors, people who "didn't wound me," who helped him grow the wings that carried him back here.

The book keeps circling back to that gesture: standing in the cinder driveway between going to die and deciding, instead, to tell you about the people and forces that formed him. The barn, the bay, the inlet, the walk down "memory's cinders", all are literal places and also stations in a spiritual physics. By the time we reach the final Fire Island sequence, when the speaker announces, "Now I set the yellow suitcase down," we realize the entire collection has been the work of opening it carefully, bead by bead, name by name, until the suitcase isn't so much emptied as transformed into light.

Illness, Time, And The Art Of Leaving Well

This is a late book in every sense: late in a life, late in a century, late in a planetary climate. Marbrook faces illness and dying without piety and without denial. In "Plaguetime," he is at once offended and amused that the earth will not "waver on its axis" without him, and yet he imagines himself becoming a nor'easter, going "stately out to sea to dance with dolphins" until his next appearance on a weather chart. Mortality here isn't a curtain drop; it's another atmospheric state, another role in the drama of matter.

"Lettest thy servant" answers the old prayer with a very contemporary tenderness.

The instruction to "be cordial as you're dying" feels almost comically modest, until you realize he means it literally: be courteous to the machines, the "pumps and poles, beeps and gravel," to the human hands around you, to the lived moments you're gathering up as you go. Death is "a rehearsal, not a splatter of indigestible notions," a reunion rather than an obliteration.

Elsewhere he is more sardonic. In "While we sleep," divinity is something we ducked because "divinity was too hard for us," so we invented gods to blame for our own cowardice. Truth, he suggests, is shy; it comes out to play "while we sleep," when our scripts fall away. Later, in "Peony on my breakfast plate," he stages a farewell that is part ecological scruple, part comedy of embarrassment, and part cosmic apology: he must be going, he says, so that "the Taconics will be okay" and swindlers in Boca Raton can rest knowing one fewer person has their number. Yet for all the jokes, the poem ends in a sobering recognition: "I came owing rent, eviction notice in hand, / I go a sob of grief, a gasp, aghast to have stayed as long as this."

Marbrook's dying is never only his own. It's entangled with melting glaciers, rising seas, pandemic time, political rot, the long after-effects of abuse. To read this book is to share his sense that our personal exits are braided into a much larger mutating system, that "we have all been waiting for the seas to rise, / and yet we wish the glaciers well."

ANGELS, MUTATORS, AND THE LONG AFTERLIFE OF HARM

If the yellow suitcase is filled with "unbelongings," a good many of them have names. A long central movement of the book is a gallery of portraits: Adrian, Sally, Mary, Alan and Jerry, Edith, Lilith, Hermes, Aisling, Nita, Dominick, Jordie, Jenny, Hank, Gus, Sherm, Purdy, Miles, and many more.

They are lovers, predators, saints, neighbors, classmates, fellow broken children, mutators of the poet's life.

What's striking is that very few of them are flatly damned or flatly redeemed. Sally, sexually abused as a child, discovers the terrible sacredness of her own body as "her melody whereby she keeps / the rivers running to the sea." She is both wounded and priestly, a guardian of "anonymity" against exhibitionists. Aisling is a "motherly predator" who turns children into werewolves; but the poem insists they "own her too," because "that's how it is when you mess with angels", abusers become caught forever in the orbit of those they harmed.

"Writ," one of the book's most searing poems, recalls a house where a boy was "chalk, pen, vessel, eraser, dildo," "used to purposes I understood / as if I had never been innocent." The imagery is shocking and exact: the child is turned into stationery and sex toy, instrument and residue. Yet the poem refuses to settle for the word survivor; it prefers a more unstable angelology. The boy is tied by a silver chord to a fallen angel; his name is "writ on salt sea," legible only as spume. Even here, where pain might justify pure rage, the poem reaches for a metaphysical exactness rather than a simple verdict.

"Mob" and "Angels" widen this meditation. The "broken angels" society tries to clip and correct, the queer kids, the misfits, the "problem children", are the very beings we will need "when the meteor strikes" to blow on our cinders with the forgiveness we never gave them. In Marbrook's cosmos, the injured are not inspirational posters; they are structurally crucial to any hope of our survival.

And then there are the mutators: friends whose presence alters the chemistry of the speaker's life, sometimes against his will. In "Mutator," he describes a man with a "twenty-mile look" who seemed to see too much, whose gaze dropped into you like a plumb bob, as if to build a scaffold from your own actions and hang you on it. The speaker wants him gone so he can breathe.

He wants to be free not only of his own secrets but of the someone-else whose daemon has been protecting this man all along. Here as elsewhere, Marbrook is exquisitely alert to the way one life is changed by the gravitational field of another.

Memory, Matter, And
The Metaphysics Of Tidewrack

Over and over, these poems insist that what we call "the physical" is neither solid nor simple. In "Tidewrack," human beings are not just debris but "matter / wet with alkahest," soaked with an alchemical solvent that remembers "previous phases" and "having come again and been ennobled." In "Glaciers," our thoughts persist under ice for millennia like pollen, ready to blossom into new civilizations once thawed. In "Foreign?" God isn't a bearded overseer but "nebulae pondering what we become / as we die for each moment / in its privilege."

That phrase, "die for each moment", captures something essential in Marbrook's poetics. He sees time not as a line but as a series of chrysalises; each second is a husk we must break, leaving behind "incalculable loss" and tools we barely know how to use. We are "majesties of memories" who have sold our grandeur out to the clock.

This is not armchair metaphysics. It is rooted in very particular landscapes: Great South Bay, Montauk, Narragansett Bay, Fire Island, Brooklyn Bridge, the Narrows. The sea, in this book, is never mere backdrop; it is a vast archive of wrecks, "sea glass / ground from the tableware of nations' wrecks," a solvent that both erases and refines. In "Darkling cradle," a piece of blue sea glass rolls at the feet of the Brooklyn Bridge, an "ocean's child" being polished down to its essentials. In "Fire Island," the speaker's leukemia becomes "rocket fuel" for a voyage to a "wedding of particles," a reunion in which he aspires to be "anonymous," just one more muon, gluon, axion in God's particularity.

Matter, in these poems, thinks. Plants lean toward certain people; wood has a will; dandelions possess more courage than fighter pilots; loosestrife and kudzu may very well have opinions about our wars and zoning laws. The point isn't sentimental animism; it's an ethical re-scaling. If we are "tidewrack," then our dramas, however intense, are part of a much older and wider metabolism.

Social Weather: Racism, Power, And The Hooligans In Brioni

Marbrook never lets his metaphysical reach become an excuse to ignore the concrete cruelties of social life. The early self-description "half-caste, bastard, dismayed" quietly marks him as a subject of racial and class othering. Throughout the book, that otherness keeps surfacing, in "Bobby," where a Black boy with green eyes sees how the dice are loaded to make him not see that "we're strung on a common thread," and in "Nether glow," where anyone who "looks like you're gonna say something real" is liable to be beaten, raped, or evicted by "hooligans in their uniforms, / their Brionis and wifebeaters."

"Condoms" is one of the collection's most ferocious social poems, recasting us as "defective condoms of Babylon / bobbling in a hurricane of self-concern," harbingers of "bastardies and motherhoods / in name only." It's obscene, funny, and deeply sad: a portrait of a culture that weaponizes sex, abandons children, and then drowns its guilt in patriotic noise.

"Heat" and "Room for you" look more closely at tribal belonging, family, nation, ideology, as a matter of turning off warmth, of "not wanting to belong to that other tribe," even to the point of poisoning their wells. The poems about boarding school ("Alan and Jerry," "Jenny," "Aisling") show how class privilege and sexual predation intertwine: boys and girls sent away to be improved become raw material for adults' secret appetites, their beauty "gemmy" and expendable.

In all of this, Marbrook's anger is precise. He's not simply railing; he's tracing how systems of power infiltrate personal memory, how the "standards" of decency and success are often the very mechanisms by which we are maimed. Yet even here, he keeps an eye on the small generosities that persist, Peachy, who listens; Bud, the quiet telescope of a boy; Miles, the journalist who decides the "wonts of wood" are more urgent than the wants of ambitious men.

STYLE: ALKAHEST, SEA GLASS, AND STAGECRAFT

What might strike you first, and keep delighting you all the way through, is the sheer strangeness and exactness of the language. Marbrook's diction slides easily between sailor's rigging (stay, tang, block, boom), bar talk, theological jargon, and invented or revived words like "alkahest," "hornswoggledom," "hiraeth." He can move from Petrarch to paper planes, from Corot to candy wrappers, without ever sounding showy for its own sake.

He has a gift for yoking the high and low in a single line: "clouds of unknowing" brush up against "Boca Raton swindlers"; a boy falls face-down on a condom as if it were a theological heresy; the sun is "a yellow splotch on an artist's smock," and we're off into an extended chain of apologies that manages to be both slapstick and metaphysical.

Metaphors in this book are rarely tidy. They fray, multiply, talk back. In "Her smock," a single blur of yellow paint becomes morning, shame, a badge of having splattered one's grief onto another's clothing. In "Lightning," storms pass "through" the speaker so completely that he becomes an impediment others resent, a transparent obstacle that still somehow leaves them "drenched and shivering."

Formally, the poems are mostly free verse, but they are anything but formless.

The long, enjambed lines often feel like thought trying to outrun itself, or like surf that keeps pushing a little farther up the beach before sliding back. Marbrook uses apostrophe constantly: the second person "you" is addressed to childhood tormentors, lovers, angels, the reader, himself. There are dramatic monologues (Hank, Gray, Fran, Nita) that could be staged almost as they stand. There are list-like litanies of roles, "chalk, pen, vessel, eraser, dildo", that read like inventories of a haunted house.

Perhaps most interesting is his own stated sense of what poetry is. In "Rest," he writes that "acceptance is poetry, / not artfulness but art." The poem insists no poem can ride the rogue wave that's coming; we are going to wreck. Our skills will not save us. The only honest art is to consent to tatter, to inhabit the sob itself rather than trying to surf above it. That is as good a description as any of the ethic that governs The Yellow Suitcase.

SUGGESTIONS ON READING THIS BOOK

I think of The Yellow Suitcase as a kind of tide pool in which an entire life's worth of wreckage, wonder, and experiment has been left behind at low tide. It is not a linear autobiography. It doesn't explain itself. It assumes, quite rightly, that you too are tidewrack, "wet with alkahest," carrying your own shards of Great South Bay, Fire Island, Brooklyn, Providence, or wherever your particular storms have landed you.

You can read it straight through and feel the narrative arcs, the return to the barn, the opening of the suitcase, the approach to Fire Island, but you can also enter anywhere: through Sally's fierce sacrament, through Bobby's green eyes, through the weary humor of "Convivencia" or the fierce clarity of "Nether glow." Each poem is a bead on a necklace that, as he reminds us, is always breaking apart to join a larger one. Loss, here, is "a vulgar swindle." Nothing essential is ever really lost; it's re-strung elsewhere.

As you read, you may notice yourself changing the way you look at ordinary things: sea glass, dandelions, cracks in the floor, the way someone sits in a waiting room. That's one of this book's quiet achievements. It keeps nudging you toward a kind of X-ray seeing: a recognition that every moment is a crossing place of particles, memories, injustices, rescues.

I never knew Djelloul Marbrook in the flesh. But after living with these poems, I feel as if I've been allowed to walk with him down that cinder driveway, to stand beside him as he weighs whether to open the yellow suitcase, whether to walk to the barn or to the bay. The fact that he chose, again and again, to open the case, to show us not just the "defiled unbelongings" but the salvors, the angels, the mutators, the sea glass, the condoms, the peonies, is, I think, a final and very stubborn act of hope.

You're holding that act of hope in your hands now. When you're ready, crack the latches. Let the bluebirds startle. Let the marigolds murmur. There's weather in here you may recognize.

Kurt Lovelace, author of
Halfway Between Everywhere
Thanksgiving, Thursday 17 November 2025

THE YELLOW SUITCASE

AWASH

The Yellow Suitcase

You wounded me. The wounds grew wings.
Here I stand in this cinder driveway,
cardboard suitcase in my left hand.
By you I mean a cyclotron of half-blind predators
and events, a collective pronoun barred
to the likes of me. By likes I mean half-caste,
bastard, dismayed, thrown up, tidewrack,
bobbing in the inlets of a dark consciousness,
not ensconced like mussels in a bank,
uncertain of wanting to be alive,
bereft of the reckless abandon of condoms
and candy wrappers.

I've come here to die,
to sit by a window facing south in a rotting barn
and die like an equation on a blackboard
awaiting erasure.
Not to be interrupted I am, not to be transgressed yet again.
And yet I don't know what to do
with this beaten valise.
Its red, black and green stripes argue not to open it,
not to spill its defiled unbelongings on the ground,
so while I'm standing here entranced
I'll tell you about people who didn't wound me,
salvors for whom I grew the wings that carried me back here
to the shores of Great South Bay.
That's what this is about, a preface
to a long walk on memory's cinders down to the barn,
to the lightning storm I hear coming,
thunder grumbling in my veins.

Plaguetime

I don't know if I'll live to prune the lilacs again,
but who of us knows if we'll make it across the street?
Did Turner live to finish Ovid? I'm offended
earth won't waver on its axis without me, offended
it might even have a good laugh at my expense,
offended and yet amused by my own hubris.
I may wind up missing nothing, being nothing missed,
but I have a feeling lately of being in someone's arms,
exhilarated and frightened, unmoored and likely
to part company with the ground, to consort
with the hurricane season, to become a nor'easter
and then go stately out to sea to dance with dolphins
and if not to forget all this at least to set it aside
until my next appearance on a weather chart.
I did nothing more important than prune lilacs
no matter what anyone said I did, and I'm sorry
I left it to a yard man this year, but I was ill
and trying to listen to my illness speak.
It's a good thing Turner left that harbor unfinished,
if that's what he did, because nothing ever is
and that we think otherwise is our disease.

Briefings

Because you wanted to hear more
you missed the import of what had been said.
Double back, listen again.
Each of you is a briefing, testament nothing's lost
or left behind.
You're long shadows of something else again
feeling the tug of being withdrawn.
Sleep in this cradle rocking among stars.
Give up your imprisoned sob,
so much like etching on a prison wall.
More is never enough, an illusionist's trick.
This, this is your report and the very first time
someone is listening with nothing else in mind
but to cherish every word, gesture, expression
and not withhold anything that might comfort you.
This is what you couldn't have
because you couldn't imagine it, love
requiring nothing of you but what you've given,
what you've already done.

Tidewrack

If life were a game of marbles,
each country a different board,
and politicians strategists,
journalists the gladiatorial mob,
we'd be tidewrack, algae and debris,
but we are instead the matter
wet with alkahest, struck through
with memories of previous phases,
of having come again and been ennobled,
of setbacks and accidents. This game of marbles
in which we're beguiled to roll
and rub against each other,
clattering to cheer and lament,
this game is the veil we must tear off
to see ourselves as far less physical
than we've been tricked to suppose.

Glaciers

Pollen.
Infectious as we are,
after millennia under ice
our thoughts blossom into cities
and country-sides, new seas, rising tides,
mocking slant slabs and pigeon-coated statues.
Infectious as we are,
pollinators, sober mornings
after orgies of our data, free
of claptrap, blather and belief,
discovered under glaciers transfigured
and transfiguring.
Dangerous, if you will, or if you won't,
dangerous in our wont to transcend
the awkward luggage of our circumstance.
Pollen,
alert as when we surrendered it
to the horror shows of funerary practice,
dangerous to anything you take comfort in,
apt to flower in untimely places,
unlikely faces, apt to rival cultivated gardens,
to celebrate what no one knows
and revel in what unfolds
like sheets suggesting orifices
on the other side of our nose.

In A Waiting Room

I think I may let you go first, if it's all right,
there's something I want to write.
It was my decision to put the benches where they are
and that decision may be as momentous
as the work of carp in reeds,
the position of the hawk in trees,
the shadow of the heron on the pond,
more momentous than the breaking news.
What I with my poor vision see
all without coveting may be
as significant as the canisters
into which we cram what little we know.
I think primal knowledge of this
herds us into societies that hurt our feet
and turns to mockery what we might have been
had we a little more respect for what can't be traded up,
something say, something like the social animal I'm not.
As you watch me totter down the hall
think what would my epitaph say
had it shone briefly in the glare? Something,
something I want to write,
maybe even something I want to right:
If I had no pride, if I were fully conscious,
you'd never hear from me.

Narrows

While I was waiting for the light to change
the city behind me disappeared
and I stood out to sea on a quartering gale,
my orders still unopened, my hopes
jettisoned to steady this bone craft as she goes
into the narrows and gulf's discharge,
up the belly's twenty-mile swells,
past the middle finger of Montauk
to the ecstasies of knowing not where
and there to gather evidence from the sea bed
of the tectonic trysts and reasons
true knowledge never shows its hand.
All is about unknowing, hallowing
uncertainties rioting behind us
as we wait for the light to change,
change our fearful insistence
we're not the sacrament that plunked us here.

Barbary Pirate

So now I speak of back when I was alive,
but isn't that like saying tomorrow where I live?
Pardon me, my sword is crescent-shaped.
Let me speak in languages come back to me unbidden
of laws I've decided not to obey,
something I negotiated with Petrarch,
a vowel some sultan ordered me
to hang on a consonant's mast
in order to sail closer to the wind,
to raid Cork with impunity and carry off
its silver chalices and its women
for exchange with northern ghosts.
Let me speak without confidence
words will not sail off the page,
dragons will not dine on them,
without any of the illusion
that props up my loitering.
Just because everything is an allusion
doesn't mean I have to revere its veil.
Let me not eschew gibberish
as if I understood all it's not,
let me trust this instrument
more than any scimitar or word.

The Necklace

If a necklace breaks apart you may think a bead is lost,
but that's the vanity you hang around your neck.
Loss is a vulgar swindle, a capital lie.
You're a proprietor of nothing,
high as you are on your own bullshit.
The cosmos is held in common
by algebra half transcribed,
each a memory a break
with hornswoggledom.

Your triumph as a child is you never imagined owning
anything more than a paper plane, a grass harp,
and then only for a moment.
You understood belonging as borrowing,
Dowd of Dowd's Inlet as a damn fool,
riches as burglary, life as the flow of memory.
When your mother gave you that who-the-hell-are-you look
it was insightful, you were right to grin.

The necklace always falls apart but only
to rejoin a larger one, and your life has been
a hard unblinking look at remorse.

Benefit Street

All is there as we left it
but for the wateriness of there.
The same Studebaker in the dawn
trundles down Benefit Street to Fox Point
for a breakfast boilermaker.
It always will, but there will always be
people who say its destination is the junk yard.

We're engaged in turning signs around,
sticking hoses in bronze horses' mouths,
making them piss weeks on end,
playing pranks on each other
until we're sick to death of them,
sick of ourselves, for that matter,
and all the while clamors scurry under the bed-stand
after pencils, pills and bottle caps;
why not eighty-seven years
and the cleaning crew?

I've been an artifact in progress since I was born.

Civilizations are lost under that table.
Well, that's the official narrative,
but I say they ply the stream of consciousness—
thought, impression, memory, encounter—
and are never put away.

Foreign?

The climates of hollows are as distinct as vaginas,
they summon our particles to consort
throughout the universe—
nothing's foreign.

We're taught to think in sames
and yet to assert our differences.

God is nebulae pondering what we become
as we die for each moment
in its privilege.

Seconds are chrysalises, husks,
and we emerge reckoning with incalculable loss
and means we don't know how to use.

God is not a vulgar anthromorph,
a demon of our imagining.

We think life's a lit fuse,
a sulky wait for an explosion
which when it comes is afterword,
but the barometric pressure of the moment
is what we're here to gauge,
the rest is television weather.

We're majesties of memories,
grandeur sold out to the clock.

Writ

In this house I was chalk, pen, vessel, eraser, dildo,
swag under mattresses, smoke of maple leaves.
Survivor I was not. Here are stocked
the sins and scents of my trespassers, the stink
of my trespasses, their vials rocking in the bathos
of my forgiveness. Survivor I was not.
A fallen angel tied by a silver chord to the boy
deposited there, the boy I too left behind, angel
of shivers and fevers and blisters, ransacking angel
whose one ambition would become to sit
before Jean-Baptiste Camille Corot's *Ville d'Avrai.*

In this house I was used to purposes I understood
as if I had never been innocent,
and because I understood, predators hated me.
But how did I understand? I worked it out in poetry,
I sweated it out in bed but never trusted bed
to keep me safe. It was no rockaway,
it was sheet lightning, thunder.
I shuttered this house against hurricanes
but not the importunings within.
My own barometer, I prayed to God to be whisked away.
You think you know my name?
It's writ on salt sea, crests of waves its diacriticals.
What speaks to you is spume.

Mob

As long as the angel's the problem child
civilizations stall while parents figure out
how to clip its wings. Earth winces, stars weep,
and good ole boys conspire with fat cats
to have a little fun at the levee.
Mercury's stuck in retrograde
as long as the child's in their clutches,
but hell's about to break loose on Golgotha.
In three days the meteor strikes
and we'll need all the broken angels we can find
to blow on our cinders in their hands
with the forgiveness we never gave them
for the sin of being different.
We'll need the otherness we despise,
and if we count on them being there,
is it hypocrisy we think ennobles us?

Rest

No poem can ride this rogue wave
out of the west's improbable womb,
no work of art, no utterance, no prayer
or any human device. It will jerk loose
stay, tang, sheet, block, boom, sail,
and leave the perfect yacht a wreck.
This oceanic sob must be inhabited
for all its fearsomeness
even if the inevitable end is tidewrack,
even if you become scrim or algae,
sea glass or something humbler,
your skills to no avail, give them up,
consent to tatter and for once accept
nothing you will help you
get on top of this or be remembered.
That acceptance is poetry,
not artfulness but art. No recognition
can be pocketed nor is it property.
Rest in this hurricane hole, this inlet
of dismay, rest, nothing's over
and there's nothing to get over on.

Lettest Thy Servant

I

Be cordial as you're dying.
Make your escape angelically.
It's a rehearsal, not a splatter of indigestible notions
and choked emotions,
a reunion, becoming whole again.
Very cordial as you're dying
so to let four walls, pumps and poles, beeps and gravel even,
let them know into whose arms you're falling.
You're taking every single moment with you,
ennobled and refined. It's only the clutter
of nomenclature you leave behind.

II

We are woven with silver thread to each other, heart and mind.
Brushing way the webs of ism we become a prism
refracting ancient light, recognitions
searching black seas.

We have eaten our own root, slashed the veil
of blood, flag, hoo-ha and lewd exhibitionism
to hear thoughts behind words, intent behind gorgeous looks
and the dizzying vacuity of entitlement.

Listen, listen to what I mean, listen to this sharp spade
turning clods of words with a flash of probity.

III

I have a friend whose blah blah blah makes me a big shot too.
So what if I like a little drinky-poo now and then?
I have big plans that might include you.
He's got money to burn, this friend, money I show him how to
spend.
You just gotta have a little faith in me.
You have to drink with these guys, you have to listen to their
lies?
Are you kidding me? I mean, are you fucking kidding me?
I'm gonna make you filthy rich, I'm telling you.

Hey buddy, I gotta go. My friend's outside.
Yeah yeah, my computer died is why I asked you for the loan.
What're you gonna do? Moan and groan?
This is a big opportunity?

Shooting the TV with a shotgun perched on your toes,
that's old hat, now we're civilized,
we drown our phones in lemonade.
And the guy with the friend who blah blah blah?
we just made him county treasurer, ha ha ha.

TIDES

A Just Dream

Was it just a dream or was it a just dream,
the great emerald wave churning cities in its lap?
The two of them in their old age sat watching
its approach, sat among the broken columns,
cracking esplanades, falling bridges, as the waters rose.
They held each other's hands. Words floated away.
And then to his right a bronze-haired woman appeared.
The old man put his arm around her
and she lifted them up to the gangway of a crystal ship.
Then she was gone and they put out new leaves,
epiphanies born of hard work on earth.
They looked down with their fingers on their lips.
Weren't we always amazed? the old woman said.
Dismayed, he said.

Belle

Never been at the center of anything
for fear of not being able to get out.
Belle, who told them I'd be one,
told them I could be rung
or wrung or whatever the hell they were thinking?
I like peripheries and penumbras,
like not letting anyone in, but once in a while
the doors of my Santa Sophia blow in
and some sultan's mare shits on my altar,
or that's how I think of it when I'm silly enough
to let someone else fuck me for a night,
only for a night and not to hang around
because my name is Belle and that should signify
something that I'm not. Centers are for members
and I don't want to be a member of anything
or anyone, but that doesn't mean I never saw an abyss
I didn't want to look in. Belle? I'm the abyss,
that's why they gave me such a presumptuous name,
so not to take me seriously lest they find me
too slippery to climb out. That's why
we give ourselves titles and names, to shirk
the dangers of knowing anything,
to celebrate our ignorance. Fuck me for a night,
did I say that? Nobody gets out of me alive,
even my own fingers hardly make it.

Never been at the center of a fire or an idea,
but I've fondled the hood and labia of them
and burst all over the window sill
at the sheer damn silliness of calling me Belle,
which is not to say I'm not pretty or even beautiful
but is to say I don't need Botticelli to testify
or the Uffizi to ennoble me. I'd scare him silly.
He'd know he wasn't supposed to blunder in,
wasn't supposed to pick up a brush
or stir his paints, wasn't supposed to speak or gesture.
He was supposed to bow his head and let me by.

Cal

Cal hadn't really lived anywhere until he was old
and from that frontier post he looked back
on the dragonflies and other hoverers without remorse.
His time as loiterer in doorways, a voyeur,
washed off him, sweat and blood in a waterfall.
He'd been their honey and noonday
witness to their gatherings.
He smiled in every bubble and read by the light
of every molecule.
Where he'd been was a matter, a matter only
of how it had ennobled him, how much
he'd consented to dance with it, to sing
not to cheer but to search for that chord
in which nothing matters but this, this moment
in which every window stands to burst,
in which the whole of civilization writes
its story on the wall, forewarning only
that each glance and utterance
was quintessential, after all.

Adrian

My bones can't lift this dead weight tonnage.
Dreams are the derricks lifting me out of bed,
swinging me around to this and that lily pad
to mark the agonizing rise of the smoky sun.

This is the life of a poem like me, and yes,
I think it's what Adrian wanted to be,
hurting too much to stay in bed
but unable to imagine another day.

Others of us were swamp gas,
but Adrian with her grand voice
was able to manage a sustained glow,
a moment boldly inhabited
and every time she looked at me
I knew she was saying, What else should they want of me?

Sally

The only thing Sally hasn't lost in bed is her sense of humor.
She calls it her melody whereby she keeps
the rivers running to the sea, not to mention her sanity.
Not that her quim conforms to her whim,
but that it's her divine rite and right to restore
what giants corrupt, and to do it savagely
or some would say devoutly. Not a habit to break
but a duty to perform if only so that others
may go on enjoying their personal Gotterdammerung.
Everything was taken away from her
and then shoved back into her while she was a child.
No priest taught her this sacrament.
She discovered how to break the giant's hand,
how to quash the glamors of wolves' eyes,
the clamors of raptors' teeth, she discovered
light in her nether vault to blind the looters
who thought they left behind a broken doll.
Only the silent boy who sat behind her,
admiring her braids, deserved her flagrant melody,
and everyone else who thought they did was wrong,
every one, and that more often than not accounted
for her unseasonable smile. Wherever he is, that silent boy
is the body and blood of her sacrament, the way
what is happening depends on her
to keep it out of the hands of exhibitionists
and their tawdry identity. She coaxed anonymity
from the matrix with her fingertips
as blue whales sing her oraise, white waters revel
and the firmament drops its gown.

Mary

The boy who chewed his leather collar,
who for all his awe of art never would imagine
anything as select as Mary Corbett's bum,
that boy made it his book of common prayer
to raise the chalice to the abyss
high over remembering Mary's kiss,
to lose his footing in the fen
as the tide is coming in, to fall face down
on a condom as if it were the heresy
of transubstantiation to Protestants, that boy
thought Jeanne Hébuterne lovelier
than Mona Lisa, though not perhaps
as lovely as Botticelli's *Spring,* and none of them
equal to Mary Corbett accosting him
in her blue beret under the marquee in Babylon.
Why must she live in Wantagh just out of reach
of everything he was to become, why,
for all his navigational skills, could he never find
West Islip again or the faintest scent
of Mary momentously slipping away?
Why does it now all seem a blackboard
being erased by the bully whom inevitably
he'd have to beat up and take the blame
for twisting the tale of the official narrative?
Or perhaps he foresaw it all in that condom in light rain
electrifying the ordinary, promising
something experimental if he grew up.
But he never did, he lingered
at the entrances of the marvelous
arguing with angels,
calling his poor reflexes judicious,
mourning for what he fled, conflating
memories into art, art being what was not lived.

Edith

1

Listen, little boy raking my leaves,
nobody told you to do this, you did it
out of your abundant alkahest.
You raked your school's driveway
and then you said to yourself why not rake Mrs. West's?
And you stood there in the maple smoke
choreographing its winding curls.
You and I are crystallizations of quests,
each of us granted more than our share
of the cosmic solvent that ennobles us.
Nobody told you to do this, nobody told me
to befriend you, but our spirits are wound
like your dancers. We are moved by memories
of our ancient metabolisms. So, come,
put down your rake, sip cocoa with me
as if I were not old and you were not young
and this is another of our weddings
along an alchemical path winding back
to a star whose name pirouettes
on the tip of our tongues, a name too orgiastic
to speak, except perhaps over cocoa
this cold November day.

2

How anticlimactic to die
having lived so melodramatically.
One should lift like dawn mist
leaving what's beneath to clarify
and not make such a thing as earth bereft.
One should see death as algebra,
reconciliation of disparities,
reunion, not farewell.
At least that's how Edith saw it
waiting upstairs for her breakfast to arrive,
and when it did all that was left
in Edith's bed was resolution, equation solved.
Vulgarities lay aside, intrusions relent, hopes subside.
The funeral had already taken place
on stairs that forgot to creak.

Lilith

Our feet offend the pointillism of the earth.
We seek to salve the wound of birth,
not to tread lightly, not to tread at all.
We choose to dissolve or to seep
between bewilderments of molecules.

Sure, talk of the wonts and ways of timothy,
buttercups and birdsfoot trefoil is okay
from a horticultural point of view,
but what of the wants of what we stomp, harvest,
mow down and slaughter?

If loosestrife, crown vetch and kudzu forbidden
to want, to feel, to—hoo boy—think?
Is that hocus-pocus, bafflegab,
or are we barefoot on more shardy ground
than we have ever cared to admit?

I learned this in spite of school,
I rescued words from gobbledygook,
but they had sticky feet, and in any case
words can be trusted only so far,
and the morning after, that's too far.

If you study photos of me as a child,
as if you had nothing better to do,
you'll notice I look as if you're lying.
That's why I could never make love well.
I stopped them in their tracks

and preferred to keep the stars in the courses,
and lovers running away, that sort of thing.
I had the effrontery to believe in magic,
not my own but that I am a beat of one great heart,
a particular kind of aught as crucial as a god,
bread and wine. I unnerved them, every one,
parent, lover, conspirator, none of them friend.
I am a particle of the light required
to cast a shadow, something like

what looks like dust or pollen pouring
through an attic window as a train rumbles by,
a bolt no one should touch,
something curiously memorable for no reason,
a rose in winter, an offense to season.

Alan And Jerry

When you're old you can farm a crack in the floor.
Constantinople falls to the young regardless of cost.
In between angels are betrayed, children lost.
If you're lucky not to have become a collectible,
not to have succumbed to hiraeth you may enter
a state of grace as a wraith and depart this place
in peace if not with blessings at least with a nod
from someone who saw in you the face of God
and was never able after to tolerate lies,
not even in the fondest eyes.

Our thoughts drifted through her like clouds.
She was the weather of our veins.
Her husband was a famous jeweler
to whom we settings must be matched and fit.
They sent their inconvenient sons to boarding school
to do hard time in bed, Alan and Jerry
in whose eyes the rest of us drowned, some gladly.
We didn't sign up for these lessons in beauty,
we didn't volunteer to be betrayed,
but we did step up to witness how gemmy
the sacrifice of innocents could be
and how complicity came so easily and played
in the crooks of the most exquisite eyes.

Hermes

Even incorrect is the wrong password for Hermes,
nor can he unsubscribe from the fix.
He is the feral cat looking in,
the wolf's eye in the dawn woods,
the nautical chart without a rose,
but when you see that thousand-yard stare
you can be sure it's this kind of shock,
recognition that the correct pass is rioting
in the o of a word messed with
at the cost of another go on earth.
Not a roulette wheel or a target or any kind
but a desperate heart beating the walls
of vulgar containment.
He doesn't want to be Hermes in fields
that have to be filled in, recipient
of what can't be unsubscribed, and if once
he did long to get in he knows now that adyta
beguile and delude, all holy of holies lie
and must be passed by as the only divine act
worthy of all this suffering.
Then the message can be delivered,
the one he is trusted not to read
or even to ask who will read it,
and all those who kept him out or initiated him
into the glitz of their purposes
he thanks without irony from his bed
knowing he has lost his life under it,
like slippers and pens and TV remotes,
like yearnings and even the occasional open door,
window left ajar, blind left up,
word sprung from its original intent,
gaze left to loiter. All is now incorrect,
reset only on pain of wanting to do this again.
Hermes will not fill the blanks. He will not submit.

Aisling

1

I wouldn't say we were happy victims,
but we were enthralled by what she made us do,
we came to know her as the second person, you,
the looming one, inescapable, as intoxicating
as our own lives were to us. Happy?
Victims? Or co-conspirators in Aisling's project
to own our fortunes, innocence corrupted, ennobled
by as many eyes as the hairs we were to grow.
Happy victims? No. But now more vigilant
than vipers in their pits, wary, capable
of picking up as many whiffs as wolves.
I would say Aisling made us werewolves
who to others' bad luck would look like sheep,
werewolves whose sleep is a masque
with second persons' demons
in the middle of the second person's night.
As for owning us, we own her too,
as it is when you mess with angels.
You think you've clipped their wings,
but there you are, the three of you, hovering
over the scene of your crime turned to runes.

2

Lightning might as well have struck them
in that window of an antique barn:
too young to have sex, having it anyway,
children shuddering in what they didn't know how to do,
mentored by a motherly predator,
left to grow up knowing about ecstasy,
looking for it again, listening to tides coming in,
trains wailing, thunder growling, lightning cracking,
hearts exploding, prospects dim, frisking others
for each other, sobbing deep within.
Neither of them so much as mentioned
what made them wolves,
but in their dreams they hunted together
and many they claimed to love they ate.

Nita

I made jerks shiver because I could,
women weren't much better.
I don't know what I was, it wasn't human,
not by any measure of my palette.
I painted my own madness in the mirror.
Flesh tones were the hardest.
I mocked the fools who lusted for me,
I lusted not for them but for their folly.
Who cares about being human or anything so careless
as to be ambushed by a name?
I aspired to be a hieroglyph on a goddess's groin,
gnosis, a gateway, not a gaping wound.
But in my old age my pants fell down
and there was my wrinkled arrogance.

Dominick

Never young at heart, he couldn't imagine being old,
not unusual in an angel, tragic in a man.
Dominick took on duty as boats do water,
his lion's eyes giving nothing away,
He was Dionysus of the Third Avenue El,
Achilles of Charlie's Bar and Grille.
Charlie's is an Irish pub now,
that would stick in Dominick's craw,
as Joe King's Rathskeller did
with its drunken West Point cadets.
Who else went home to chat with snow leopards,
to correct polar bears' dentures,
inveigh against the cripple Roosevelt
and sing the praises of Walter Lippmann?
Only Dionysus the taxidermist,
Achilles of the assault on Reds.
Dominick lived in a house of molds—
snow leopards, bears, tigers, not a one
as fierce as him.

Jordie

Jordie's hardcore face disguises his open mind.
Just as well. It discourages triflers.
But the real problem's his silence.
The pretty girls who sat in front of him at West Islip
called him Silent Boy. He never said a word to them,
but they knew he liked them. He was their rock.
They counted on him not to pull their pigtails
or play tricks on them. But he scared them,
and sometimes scared himself.
The older he got the more he remembered his face
on someone else's skull, someone he mourned,
so he set out to see who it bothered
and whether they could stand his emerald gaze.
His mother couldn't, his stepfather couldn't,
but those two pretty girls liked how it made them shiver
and taught him how it was going to be.
He wasn't going to be a fat cat or a lawyer,
he was going to swim underwater and blow things up,
he was going to get hurt and have to part his way
through zombies in a nightclub who,
unlike Jordie, never figured out
each moment's a cyclotron, an ampersand,
and God knows what comes out,
but it bears little resemblance to what went in.
We've died so many times before we die
our mourners ought to dance,
and if you plunge into his fixed stare
you might just stroke off with him to an atoll
where time's a plain doughnut dunked
in a cidery recognition all there really is is now.

Jenny

It was necessary to drop the cellar door on Jenny's head
to break her habit of running him down and peeing on him.
In the Spirit of '76, you understand.
And just as necessary for Jenny to conclude
only a gay boy would be so caddish.
Now you understand a little about how it was,
the tart air of the bay washing over their feverish attempts
to slip the shackles they clamped on each other,
the predatory adults, their copycat victims,
and the impediment of not knowing anything about sex
except some of them were different down there
and that difference would devour them
if they didn't learn how to be little shits in a hurry.
If it hadn't been for the bay and Fire Island beyond
with its quim pulling ocean in
and exuding what there weren't enough clams to clean
the boarding school would have been picked apart by ravens
for nests on telephone poles and trees,
and the children would have been spirited by dolphins
down the road and out beyond Montauk to die laughing
at the clownishness of what had happened to them.

Fran

Fran heard shouting in another room
and when he got there found himself asleep,
the walls in back of him cut away,
and all those who'd tinkered with his mind
and spelled his sex with an h
peering in on him. Fran took his headphones off
and heard whimperings of the dead
some of whom had wished him well.
How could he be out there and yet herein,
a hurricane looking for its tail,
toiling in an interval called life?
Something about his hearing strays
into dimensions lost to sight,
something about his sight smells
illicit fragrances forbidden to illuminati
because they belong too much and like it
at the expense of the next damned thing.
If Fran has sinned it's for taking too much in
and looking too warmly and too long
at those who bathed in his every ill.
Did he think to transfigure them
or merely borrow their materials?
What alchemies did he perform,
what actors did he wed that he should set aside
languages' prosthetics and run
to the aid of strange creatures' nightmares?
Fran doesn't choose to be Frank or Francis
because only Fran, pronounced slowly, leads to none,
none of this, none of that, none
of anything but what he should become.

Raine

Raine understood herself as dusk,
creaturely in impenetrable ways,
not a temple, an alembic or mortar and pestle,
but a fatal unknowing suitable to her name,
a child who could not be beguiled,
a woman whose gaze could not be distracted,
a portal more transformative than death
and therefore someone to be removed,
and yet where to go? What trace to leave,
if any, in whose eyes to disappear?
That was the only question about her,
in whose eyes were fleeting respite from the glare
so that she might repair, and once in a great while
she found them and they went on wearing her
in their faces, summoning ancient friendships,
appearing as old lovers to strangers,
unnerving them as one would expect
parting pond mist, juggling swamp gas,
rowing in the dusk with no intention
of returning to a hearth.

Hank

Hank, are you just gonna sit here and watch her die
singing in a high hard pitch of her fear
of good ole boys and their clubbiness
in this improbable mountain fast, just gonna let
that impossibly vivid girl sing herself to death
with a kind of imam's prayer in this dark hall
where the waiters look down with cold faces
on you and your ridiculous orders, just
let her try to push that ornate carriage out of here
knowing she ain't gonna make it
and whatever you're gonna do it ain't up to you
to save your own ass, not this day, no how,
not hardly up to you 'cause there's no way
you ought to have made it up here,
not in your condition of getting along
just so you don't have to be yourself
and sing your own death song. Hank,
are you gonna help her out or is she too vivid
for watery eyes to bear, too sturdy in her resolve
to say what you always knew, that good ole boys
are out to not only kill them but some of us too,
some of us women, us children, us hard heads
who look cold waiters in the face and pity
preachers' wives and piss in pitchers of Kool-Aid,
yeah, us too, us foreigners born and bred

down in the hollows who occasionally wander
up here to places like this, places cut
out of granite where whatever's going on
ain't hardly like you was taught
and people do odd things that get them killed.
Hank, what the hell are you gonna do
even if you end up out back in a dumpster?
If I had to bet I'd say you'll think of something,
something that may ring true as her song.
Isn't that what they always feared in you,
that some day you wouldn't just sit there
and then there'd be an irreparable tear
in the mountainside, rumbling that wouldn't quit,
and you and your sister sitting on the porch
watching the whole goddam thing end?

Bud

Bud's concerns were always others,
he was himself a telescope
extended, naked, retracted, swathed,
matte finished, never shiny, capable
of scanning horizons shrouded in belief,
ready for a child to find in a turtle's nest
or in some broken doll's lap
or dropped along the bank of a cloudy inlet.
Bud looked made to be lost, glass and mirrors
not meant for birds or ships, too bold
in his quiet way to be of any practical use
unless of course you wanted to see
a truth your life conspires to deny.
He knew he would have to be stamped out
like dandelions on a golf course,
but he didn't think himself doomed to see,
rather he thought himself a lightning strike
in waiting, a one-off boy
who only accidentally might grow old,
and that would be a kind of failure.

Gus

Gus is not entitled to be tired,
there is no license to be him
looking from the outside in.
His job's to be a sparrow caught in crosshairs
of drunken hunters who need to look down,
a foil of people who need to take offense.
Hapless offender to the happily offended,
Gus is a shapeless night visitor,
troubler of sleep. Is it yours, this sleep
or does it require the article?
Gus the insignificant is the pain in your side,
and the good thing about you, perhaps the only good thing,
is that you've handed your instincts over to derelicts
like him, washed up on your south shore,
in your tidal inlets and secret coves,
somewhere between Babylon and Bay Shore.

Sherm

Sherm's okay if he doesn't eat
and talk is held to celebrations.
Life's for him the icing on vomitous cake.
and children are broken-wing sparrows.
His strength is never wanting to get in,
never seeing belonging worth the cost,
so what is there to do but cultivate trees
and scuttle away like dry leaves?
Making himself felt is vulgar,
feeling himself problematic,
and that's refinement beyond any pale.
The flapping of flags is too noisy,
belief a game of greed, containment
a ruse, blood hyperbole, and all
that's trustworthy forbidden,
the sort of things only children see.

Purdy

All civilization, all her experience of it
comes down to not peeing in her pants.
She hoped to associate herself with towering ideas
that might transcend her creatureliness,
but now she smells the ammonia of defeat.
Purdy had been corrected for her inappropriate smile
and now in old age that prodigal returns.
Her name, an appeal to God, stands in the way
of leaving this damned place composedly.
She tells the nurse she doesn't remember it.
Her childhood floods in, maybe she'll drown in it.

Neild

We're all dying, more or less,
and while an exuberant old age might seem gross
overreach an emboldened one might do.
Neild was sitting on a bollard looking out
on Narragansett Bay when he said this
to a curious herring gull, thinking it a better audience
than platitudinous friends.
Look at it this way, somewhere a craven child cringes
in a closet of the mind, here's as good a time as any
to take the little fink for a stroll
through all he thought cringeworthy,
buy him a hot dog maybe, or some ice cream,
and encourage him to look more in the face
than his parents ever did.
No, I'm not saying make a stoic of him,
I'm saying credit him with a little class.

Miles

Miles thought it better to study the will of wood
than overthink the latest predicament,
the wonts of wood more urgent than the wants of men.
The plants in his shop leaned towards him
like fond adepts. He didn't know what to say,
and that in a journalist is the first step
towards redefining the news.
His career was the price he paid for understanding
what we call the news is the ruse of ambitious men.
He knew a lot and all he knew was not
as important to him as what he yet might know.
Overthinking, he told a friend, is hubris,
it can get you killed especially in bed.
Miles had no idea how holy he'd become
and that's why his true mourners
were the objects in his shop, the dandelions at the door,
and a few old souls who could not
imagine a world without him. For them the news
is that we're never without each other
no matter how long it takes for that particular starlight
to arrive at our feet in the copse
where we've chosen to catch our breath.

Armin

I'll never climb up to Benefit Street again,
never turn right to the Fox Point dives or left
to the school of art, but here's what Armin said to me
when stout boilermakers snookered him out of his data:
I think we're ecstasies of invisible ink deposited
in the interstices of all the shit we put up to congratulate
ourselves. Oh, and I'd like to fuck your wife.
I'd had enough of showboats. I was a poor young sailor,
he was a graduate philosophy student at Brown.
I liked and hated what he'd said.
I wouldn't be able to shake it out of my head.
Much as I liked him and knew he was flirting with me,
I got up and left him to his superiority
and never spoke to him again. I walked home that night
in the company of rum-runners and slavers
who'd staggered up from the docks like fumes.
Invisible? Better than that, written in indelible ink.
Polish your bar with that.

Myron

It scuttled away like a leaf on dry pavement.
He couldn't get into it. There he stood,
a naked contraption, his body looking on
from the tree line, mocking him,
like a girl bedeviling a love-struck boy.
He wasn't quick enough or big enough
or small enough. It didn't fit,
it wasn't made for him, and if he could
he would have gladly found the one it fit
and introduced them, if only not to shiver
in the cold, if only to leave more thoroughly
than that leaf. It seemed he'd been indentured
to a carnival, a freak show. Then lightning
cracked the night sky open and he saw
he didn't need the costume at all.

Robin

Robin lives in the species solitude of a lone goldfish.
You hold it against him, this ruined grace
of the already dead. Starve him,
boil him on a radiator,
flush him down the toilet, it doesn't matter,
he has the look of something seen
your whole get-up is about denying.
Robin in his cheap bowl must be killed
even if you bought it and put him in it.
He knows this about you more than you
and can't be forgiven for it. There is no forgiveness
for his species, and yours is cursed
by these fatal encounters with cadmiums
that eat their containers and poison glaciers.
You've made yourself less than you were
regarding him. Better you shake snow-globes.
You tried to molest him and found him impenetrable.
Your fingers will never be warm again.
He made of you a kind of necrophiliac,
your life an abandoned cemetery.
Where has Robin gone that he can't be wiped off
the instruments you used on him,
your nether duds, your brightest lies,
where has Robin gone that you hear him breathing
as ineradicably as if he'd been made for you?

Vladimir

Vladimir crossed three states to collect Irish moss
to marbelize paper with a wooden skewer
because he thought good poems deserved it,
and when a friend found in such preciosity
a hint of incest Vladimir asked,
why should brother and sister not dehisce
a whiff of conspiracy against the wiles of category.
Why is such refinement scandalous
as if art itself similarly offends us,
and didn't such a vehicle presume
society as waypoint, buoy marker,
or might it be better to say a book's forlorn
that's not a compass rose?
Vladimir longed to know how to operate
every letterpress from Kelsey Excelsior
to Heidelberg and by this knowing to celebrate
every dot of ink. He wanted to pay the debt
of the big picture to every detail, to prompt
paper, poem, font and ink to rise to each other's challenge,
and if the scent of that is too profane
the dionysian might be persuaded to defer
to blind descent into the holy of holies.
There's a wee market for a four-thousand-dollar book
and what with print-on-demand and Amazon
his might be thought a fool's errand
but at very least it would be redolent
of headier heavens than Mont Saint Michel's floating
on the clouds. It would be absurd
in the manner of the Sermon on the Mount
and the Cloud of Unknowing, mad
the way a poet is writing his way through junk
to the incomparable, and there would be Vlad
to help him do it, to hold open the meticulous gate,
Vlad who longed to hold the logos in his hand,

Courtney

Starlight's persnickety as to how it falls,
shit-faced ornery about what it wants.
It doesn't fall on you like it falls on me.
That's how I see angels dance around you.

And that's only half of what Courtney knew
about the boy. He saw people perform profane acts
in the boy's atmosphere.

They changed each other's lives, these two,
changed them accidentally as stars do,
or as purposefully, it's up to you.

Starlight and moonshine concoct
symphonies out of scientific fact,
and there wasn't much more Courtney cared about
or heard, except this city boy and his decrepit bike.

Come sit with me on this here rock, boy.
Here 'em? 'Course you do, is why you're all abuzz
with angels guarding you in your glade
from the circles of devils in the dark.

The boy said nothing, firm in the knowledge
this old drunk was God. Goat farmer,
crazy coot, yeah, devils might say that,
but the boy, lugged up from Manhattan
by other kinds of drunks, knew Courtney
had been there waiting for him all along,
and Courtney, he knew the boy heard stars too.

In the city you can't see them for the lume,
you can't hear them for the cackle
of buying this and selling that, but a precious few
saw remnants of the music, obscure
and obvious as dandelions in Central Park,
a precious few with haunted faces
who lived in priceless emeralds.

Cliff

Cliff is a sailor, clutter his enemy,
Women loose cannons.
People and other granny knots offend him.
He swigs white lightning in bell jars.
It makes the zigzag scar on his face even whiter
and scares intruders away from a secret—
he draws like Parmigianino.
No one in his life is as useful as a monkey fist
or as satisfying as boatswain's lace,
and yet the sketchpads in his berth
are peopled with angels, mermaids,
nymphs, sylphs, goddesses, prophets, saints,
the sort of beings he encounters under bridges,
in culverts, alleys, doorways, urban jungles—
Cliff's Persepolis, capital of his sensibility,
the homeport he'd never tell the Coast Guard about,
its citizens being as reliable as tangs and blocks,
cleats and bollards, and therefore renegade
wherever the house is rigged.
No, you wouldn't know from looking at him
he's more inclined to think better of you than you of him,
but only if you've given up strutting around.
You have no clothes around him.
damned hard to make a living, that sort,
which is why it's fortunate he had a grandmother
who saw that one thing about him
and left him enough money to get by with it.
If you asked him who she was he'd say a selkie,
and the more you knew of him the more you'd be inclined
to believe it, and one night in his cockpit,
the sea bellying up his boat, white lightning
cracking in your brains, he just might show you
her portrait sitting on a rock off the coast of nowhere,
her hair indicating the direction of the lies
to which Cliff was born contrary.

Lloyd

Nothing there to be naked.
Nothing clings, sticks or lingers.
He's poised to be a toss of bones.
We whistle through him in the night,
windows rattle, we wail as if to leave ourselves behind.
Stations pass like words spoken. We dare not look back.
Has he made it to the barn, that trudge
that began when we first noticed melancholy,
or did it prove too perilous, and where do we stand now?
What is the forensic evidence Lloyd existed?
Bones that could be traced to ephemera,
rags in trees, failure to meet payroll,
matters left to vultures?
Why did he let us pass through him
as if he never had been there,
why were we not waylaid, arrested,
why was he not allayed?
We called him Lloyd, understanding
we could have called him anything
and it wouldn't matter. He was not to be detained,
and I think it wise to think this farmer,
for lack of any other name, a night train to Montauk
that couldn't bother to stop.

Angels

Johnny and Christina are angels.
No shadows or wobbly tenses.
No one in this town seems to remember them,
and when I ask their older sister she asks me not to ask,
and that's how I know they're watching over me.
The more I look for them the more I know
I came here to this planet looking for them.
They're the cause of my nostalgia
and every once in a while I see them in someone's eyes
and they see them in mine.
I never thought I was babysitting kids, I knew
who they were and they drew
whatever divinity I had in me to them
so that I never counted on them being where they should.
They had their own light behind them,
they didn't need the sun or the moon
or any of our devices, and when I ask about them
I shake this town limb to limb
and might even get myself killed for it,
but that's how I've lived, rattling the available chagrin,
and that's how I know Johnny and Christina are angels
watching over me.

Peachy

Peachy listens, others talk,
and far ahead when hanky comes to panky,
Peachy sifts debris and reasserts the necessity
of silence to the matrix in which sound breathes.
Peachy is a reflecting pool before the Taj Mahal of meaning,
the contradiction of yak,

Hard to say what made Peachy this way.
Flannery O'Connor could tell us.
Count yourself well honed to know it, if not refined,
if only because you can rest in Peachy's silence
and even be at peace with yourself.

Gordon

He didn't deserve any of it,
the good the bad the obloquy between,
but he knew it was important to incinerate
beliefs and lay their ashes on the indifferent sea,
not so much as to become more seaworthy
—they had, after all, made good ballast—
as to put on more sail and pitchpole
into the deep on which he'd been walking
just as Jesus told him he could do.
That's why he rocks like a sailor, not because
of twenty-mile rollers and slippery decks.
He was born to walk on water, knowing
it didn't signal some kind of miracle, it meant
being fully aware that what goes on below
deserves more respect than what we think we know.

Karl

Karl leaves things behind
as if he wishes to be remembered.
A tattered shirt is his pyramid,
a frayed jacket his Parthenon.
We're inclined to call it a foible,
forgetting we shed hair and follicles
and particles of ourselves that bathe
in the sweat of stars.
The toe tags we assign each other
reassure us far too much.
Everything burns behind us
one second to the next,
all is new before we blink.
This is the grandeur that we dread.
We magnetons hang Karl's chrysalises
on our doorknobs for him to fetch
at his convenience, but he is gone,
we are gone, ignorant of being
an infinite string of surprises.

Jock

You can't call anybody at three in the morning
to tell them you're dying, not if you're sober,
not if you're trying to go out decently.
Does anybody really care, do you,
or is it only recently you see
the importance of just sitting here
listening to your red blood cells
deliver oxygen to what so euphemistically
you've called your heart as if
it had been anything but a bilge pump
keeping you afloat when your corroded sea cocks
let briny recognitions in? Do you
want to dial someone's number,
having so recently discovered your own
stored in a dead brain cell? Not if you're sober,
not if decency is more important to you
than other ways of knowing who you are.
You're certainly not your name, serial number,
credentials, birth certificate, Wiki entry,
all that blather that hardly got you by
the last checkpoint. You're more like wine
from a cracked amphora seeping
into the ground of a strange garden,
the clock's ticking meaning nothing to you,
nor the light under the door, nor the sky
in the east turning pink once more.

You've been thinking about jongleur Jock juggling
hoops and pins and balls and blaming
someone in the audience when
one of them falls, you namely, blaming you,
exiling you from the all too warm embrace
of a friendship in which you failed to deliver
something you couldn't figure out, thinking
how the air seemed to collaborate
with him to keep his distractions airborne
until, that is, he noticed that you noticed
somebody had to account for what went wrong,
what always goes wrong when the curtain sticks
halfway up or halfway down
and the pulleys are revealed, the scampering
stagehands, the ropes and weights,
the essential stagecraft of the thing, the fact
it was a thing and not a being after all.
7 11 21 was Under the statue

Anne

Anne's the only girl who ever sat on my lap.
It was the first time nothing was the matter.
If absence of matter proves a black hole
maybe that's why we fall in love, to prove
something's there that's going to change
the terms of our existence, a kind of lens
that lets us see we've made too much of it,
it being how we matter. That's what Anne
came to mean to me—salvific erasure.
Like all things that fall into black holes
we had to break up. Aghast, we swore
to meet on her 21st birthday under the statue
of William Tecumseh Sherman in the park.
I didn't keep that noon date, and if she did…
well my life's a bit misshapen by that if.
Anne kissed the name off my lips,
it loitered in the shade, life became
a matter of waving it away. Nothing
can ever be so truly given as that sweet,
that tremulous namelessness.

Stosh

Stosh is trying to sleep.
Daylight, playing the role of life, keeps intruding.
He'd understood looking after his sister,
but then there was this thing about growing up
and strangers weren't so friendly anymore.
Perhaps if Maryna had accompanied him on the journey
it would have been all right,
but she liked him fixing her pink bike
and didn't seem aware of her attractions
to boys not like Stosh.
Perhaps? Perhaps is a conspiracy of ravens
setting out from a bell tower at dusk.
What disturbs his sleep is the ruse insisting
civilization pry the cracks of slumped dimensions.
Maryna was supposed to keep
the draperies up against the light,
but her feet got stuck in the muck
of beauty torqued counterwise, winched
against the usual expectations, even his own.
Stosh is not stuck, he just wants this to be over,
whatever it is, whatever over means,
and tonight, for no particular reason, he believes
the ravens won't come back.

Gray

I had the urge to panic girls with snakes,
I wasn't interested in them at all.
Their nubile mojo slipped away,
as I got rich their supple mojo slipped away.
The perfect girls grew up, slipped away.
They left me standing there, snake in hand,
grew up as if they always knew
I wouldn't, grew up in defiance
of my insistence they remain enthralled
by my power play, and on the empty baseball diamond,
snake slithering away,
I saw I had already had my moment.

Bobby

Jam or jelly, I don't know,
I'm not sure of differences at all
because the more I look the more I see
the dice are loaded to make me think
we're not strung on a common thread,
we're not as incestuous as hell, heresies
of fatwa and bull, diatoms of the sea.
They call me Bobby because Robert's a white guy.
He plays catcher, but he can't run.
The green eyes in my black head
see how we constellate. Robert sees rogue twinklers.
I see our shared two-leggedness,
he sees individuality. I like Robert, he likes me,
but not enough to date his sister.
He thinks identity's destiny, I think he's full of shit.
But, as I say, I like Robert, he likes me,
and that could get me killed.

Frank

The last time Frank felt well the ice carped
about the ambition of his calligraphies
and he came to understand surfaces crack
even before a hint of spring and he'd always
have to skate faster to avoid falling in.
He waited to see stars splatter, he smiled
to know his winter would never end
and the importance of being thin
was to the ice the same as it was to him.
Here's the truth he couldn't find
in nearby Great South Bay
or in books and certainly not in looks,
something's always breaking up,
parting company with itself,
scarring over the weight of passage overhead,
and he himself was not unlike it,
flashing, scribbling on this cold papyrus
pulled open by priestly shades before the moon.
I'm the pen of a crazy woman, he thought,
and someday this scroll will snap shut.
People will say spring's arrived, they'll celebrate,
and I'll sit over there by that ledge
breathless for having grown old so fast.

TIDEWRACK

Without Your Witness

How can you be safe in bed
hauling out to a climactic sea
where the sky is always red,
not any one but the one
where you were left for dead
and a thief made off with the spark
given you when you were an angel
and asked to witness this awhile,
this that now you think depends
on you to witness it in all
its treacherous splendor? How
can you be safe in bed
bereft of when you were an angel,
bewildered to have been asked
to come here so unguarded,
every bed an unfastening boat
hurtling back from flood stage,
you lashed to the helm like a corpse?

Mutator

The daffodils are up and he's still around.
I'm entitled to a few years without him.
I let him under my skin, I confess to that.
He didn't belong, not the way I do,
he of that twenty-mile look as if he saw
something no one else could see,
and that's intolerable in decent society.
It's a charlatan's game. I hate him for it.
It's essential he be gone so I can breathe,
so I can live not as if I'm hiding something.
I'm sure you'd understand, I could make you,
if you'd looked into his eyes and felt
that plumb bob drop down below your gut
as if he planned to make a scaffold
of all you'd done and said to hang you on.
The goddamn daffodils are up and he's still
in the social media faking decency.
I'm not his dark secret, someone else is,
and what rankles me the most is
I feel that person looking down on this glade
in which his drawn-out life chews my foot
and holds me here, waiting for worse to come,
looking down with a thin-lipped smile,
careful not to step on me, pitilessly.
I think the bastard's always had this daemon
looking after him. That's how foreign
he's always been, so what good did my tribe do me,
having had to deal with this mutator
I once so precipitously called my friend?

Her Smock

The sun's a yellow splotch on an artist's smock. I apologize.
God knows for what, but it seems appropriate.
Spell morning with a u. Apologize
as if you'd known what to do.
I could have called it a frock, not just to rhyme
or anything brash like that, but to suggest en fleur,
something louche or even incestuous.
Patients thank the nurses for the slightest things,
what do poets have to be thankful for?
For knowing poems are stagecraft in small doses
in the forlorn hope of writing one
that completes its orbit around the sun
that flares out from everyone? I apologize
for my fat rutter and calculations, for the latitudes
I allowed myself, the inconveniences I as gnat
caused the spheres. Patients thank the nurses
as they'd taken time from their busy schedules
to stick needles in and cluck dire vital signs.
Poems are stagecraft for one that's in us
that can't be coaxed from the dressing room,
that having eyed the audience once or twice
would rather skulk or fuck hot shots. Apologize
for having splattered like an egg on her smock.
I have the audacity to write about it,
to describe the color and suggest the morning fog
is an inappropriate shroud for the night before.
Thankful for a nod on the way to the john,
a paper bracelet purporting to be all I am.
Splattered, clumsy me, as if I'd cracked myself
and expected her to wear me as a badge.
Spell morning with a u, choke on your own sob,
shit black grief, as if you'd known what to do,
known all along and were just pretending
little pitchers have big ears and adults know better.

Room For You

Do you think there'll be any room for me,
anywhere to come and go? What I mean by this
is that while he was incinerating in his Spitfire
his daughter was back in America running down
a little half-caste boy and pissing on him
and the guy in the Messerschmitt who shot him down,
his wife was fucking a party functionary
on a grand estate
the very moment the little boy drowned
between the legs of the girl, and if that was how
it was going to be, all these flukes havocking
a decent mind, was any Britain or Germany
worth saving, was there any America in which a boy
could be half of anything, free to turn around
and not look into someone's crazy eyes
and smell the stink of mindlessness?
Room for you? There isn't even room for dandelions
which is why they're more courageous
blooming out of pavement than those pilots.
I think her piss made him nearsighted.
Lights looked like dandelion pods.
What would the Spitfire pilot have thought of that,
or the Messerschmitt man? If there were going to be flukes
why couldn't they have survived to be asked?
How might they have felt about the courage of dandelions?
Would they have been any comfort to the boy?
Couldn't Barthes have taken time to consider this,
or Heidegger? Jung at least laid a stone in its honor.
And if there are no coincidences, only simultaneities
and pairings, aren't we all still in the cockpit,
behind the gunsights, smelling the burning oil,
watching the Spitfire spin into the channel,
still in the moment when the girl peed, the boy drowned,
havocking, unable to turn around?

Spires

Our house is chockablock with things,
it longs to send us to the dump,
to dispatch itself according to the positions of the sun
and the urgencies of the stars, it longs
to be free of the toxins and claws of our clinginess.
It groans with this and that and et ceteras
to which we've felt entitled
while secret knowledge has set in
they're crutches for the lame.
I want to see the camera shudder
with the ecstasy of shadow's dance with light.
I want to see it break out of being shuttered in
and that's how we might collaborate with the plot
to redefine the dump as a great stonehenge
where lords and ladies dance themselves away
never having been received
in buckinghams and balmorals, crowns and gowns,
scepters and sycophants, or any such encumbrances.
Meanwhile we'll settle for dead reckoning
between one thing and another,
between mechanics and quick fixes,
settle for navigating fog, anchoring
offshore before docking to the spires
of our most joyous imaginings.

Melancholy

The house shook like stage props,
as if it had enough for one place
in the same way there are only so many looks
one face can bear, so many books
one face can bare, and if you look hard
faces are shook scenery, scarves in the wind.

No use to ring the doorbell or go
through any of the motions a camera
might record—this is the kind of intimacy
seen only once at dusk like a weasel
crossing the road. You smell of it,
and God knows who that will attract.

I've seen this kind of melancholy in the young,
in the old, not for the Taj Mahals we never see,
but for the books we never read, the faces
that elude us, light in which we hoped to bathe,
currents in which we hoped to swim, certainty
of expulsion from heaven en route to hell.

Squat

Curtains in the wind, souls loitering
in a moldy squat. What is real?
If they knew, they'd succumb
to the tattering, nattering past.
Lace curtains sewn to be passed through,
arabesques in dusty air resentful
of eyebrows that detain them.
Here he encounters his soul,
and as long as she insists on her privacy,
as long as she forbids rooms to him
he works the place like prevailing wind,
converses with it as rot and rust, insists
on watching her pee and perform
more skillful acts as if there's something
he must wrest from her, something belonging
to her too much that he must pilfer,
and she grows younger and more flirtatious
when she ought to be a derelict crone.
Neither death nor limbo nor afterlife,
this is an indecency too long postponed,
a dance children would have worked out
had not adults lifted their coverlets
exposing them to orange profanities filtered
through scented panties hung over a bulb,
panties seeming to him the veil
behind which his soul hid, luring him
to a cynosure he's too old to appreciate.
Curtains in the wind, souls uncertain
how to let go, words spilt on polished surfaces
that beguiled him into this, this what
if not wantonness?

Lightning

Lightning tries the seams of the house,
thunder breaks its legs. This is how I know what's coming.
Wildflowers madly dance. I will dissolve in water.
I will swirl counterclockwise
in the black hole of my contemplations
and seek kindred particles in distant places.
I came here a remnant, incomplete.
I gave shreds of myself away,
and there never was a time
you couldn't see a storm through me
as if were an impediment
keeping you from the other side,
something you couldn't get around
without showing your papers
or having your pockets picked.
In this way I was born to your resentment,
whatever you needed from me,
and no matter how I tried to get out of your way
you would be drenched and left shivering,
transformers flickering out,
darkness taking hold, both of us grief-stricken
in that rose instant when gravity lets go.

Darkling Cradle

Motion's child, that's me,
rolling, rolling in a darkling cradle,
a blue sea glass caper at the feet
of the thunderous Brooklyn Bridge,
dreaming in my duvet of foam
between Williamsburg and Chinatown,
what and where, here and there, this and that.
I don't need eels' nest or octopuses' cave,
this briny lap of vanities will do.
I was a bright container on a captain's table,
a flask, a bowl, an addendum hurled in a fit
of acquisition strutting as the state of things.
Take no pride in sentience, humans,
you don't know what it is, all you think is fallacy.
Rock me, dolphins, polish me for another round.
I'm almost ground to my essentials.
Sing to me, whales, sing to this ocean's child.

Condoms

We're the defective condoms of Babylon
bobbling in a hurricane of self-concern,
logos of the spent, commandos sent
to come ashore to disrupt the imaginings
of children, scum bags to be blunt,
betrayers of someone's hapless cunt,
harbingers of blasted lives, no-no's,
fathers of bastardies and motherhoods
in name only, memories washed up
on shores of indifference, urgencies
put aside for the war effort, torn
authors of the low-born and grievous,
signatures of those who leave us
for the best and worst of reasons
to an eternity of squally seasons.

Trace

You're not anyone you ever depended on,
not a bit. You're a certain way,
a consciousness beyond imagination
bound to marry encounters
you thought important to document.
Do you now, do you think it urgent
to mark your trail? Wouldn't it be better
to evaporate, knowing
you're the few moments you gave your all
to someone who understood,
and now you're the fragrance of it,
divine loiterer ascending a shudder of leaves?

Heat

He turned off the heat,
he being someone you want distance from,
and that's the other side of belonging,
not wanting to belong to that other tribe.
That's how you turn off the heat,
and with a little prod you might even poison
the other tribe's wells.
It's not about ethnography or patriotism
of any of that blah blah blah,
it's about fearful you and your mother's accusative tit.

Nether Glow

Wanna piss off the hooligans in their uniforms,
their Brionis and wifebeaters, wanna piss 'em off?
Just look like you're gonna say something real,
look like you saw what you saw,
look like you know what they really mean,
is how to piss 'em off. Look like you,
like you're not the dumb ass you oughtta be,
that'll piss 'em off, get you beaten, get you raped,
and certify your place as godsend of the world,
daemon among demons, emerald
to all the trembling elements that quake
at the idea of being ennobled by the likes of you.
They know what you see standing there
in the middle of the room shedding despicable light
and they'll make you pay for it if they can
in their soiled costumes that dazzle the press,
and you, you're less than dazzled because
you see that nether glow in the cracks
of settled matters. You can't help it,
so you're gonna get a beating or a bad divorce,
a termination or an eviction notice.
You're gonna get it because you know what it is
and they're moving heaven and earth to deny it.
You'd be a goddam immigrant, one of them,
if you could trace your ancestry back to Plymouth.
You'd be an outsider because you see inside out,
and the worse is yet to come, you have to testify
at the trial of the standers-by, the Pilates
who washed their hands of your ordeal.

Convivencia

I can build a convivencia with things I can no longer do,
I can tickle continents with waves of my nostalgia.
Talk drifts like snow across bleak highways.
Dreams wear bloody clothes.
Things lose their uses.
I am too light to stay.

I have always made Cordobas of loss, Qaballahs of fear,
eaten bitter almonds for trauma, retched gibberish
in the maw of bare-toothed day, kept tribes at bay.
But even if I'd drained the hubris out of it
it wouldn't equal a bluebird's cheer.

Onteora Lake

I remember the loons
crying like sisters in other rooms,
copperheads' reach, rubbers, crushed beer cans,
disregard ominous as dusk, toiling creatureliness
alongside the jangly pickup culture of Route 28.
It got into my marrow like toll-booth pleas
to runaway wives and absconding husbands,
cancerous, a camp ill-pitched by a dying lake
that would somehow serve itself up
decade after decade, a warning unheeded,
something to get over that got over on me
and now savages my blood. We don't know what we see
because we don't know it's like Manet's *Tarring the Boat*,
a portal to be studied at measured distances.
That is the tragedy of our disregard,
that we don't even see it when it's painted for us.

Vanishing

(JMW Turner, *Ovid Banished From Rome*, Yale Art Gallery)

Gone to live where Turner found Ovid banished
and nothing is assertive.
It may be said I hang on a wall at Yale
admired by Courbet's Liberté,
I say I'm off to learn how to vanish
and so doing how to be my own sun
warming people on the golden quay.
It may be said this is a late Turner experiment,
I say it's Turner knowing what to do,
positing us as tips of mink brushes,
the darknesses in between
illusory as everything we've made.
No more vulgar desperation
or fretting over a world without me.
Turner turned the key for me.

Parallelograms

If I had to write on the back of this I'd say
we never said the important things, never trod
dangerous ground that could have led
to parallelograms of light transporting us
from one delight to another. Instead
we made marginal notes to help us insure
emeralds just before they're lost. We haunted
manuscripts as if they're crypts with loss
so powerful it deafened us to the pleas
of worthy ones around us and allowed
broken promises to surround us
in impenetrable woundedness
because the back of this whateverness
is a wilderness we had no courage to explore.

Homer

(In honor of Milman Parry)

What, no hirsute Homer to celebrate,
no blind homeric demigod to name,
just a spool of gifted nobodies,
a mere civilization of illiterate singers?
Who concocted Homer and his gods?
It matters only to half-blind tribalists.
The unsung compelled to sing,
revise, refine, ennoble, they matter.
We're their story, they're ours.
We're not imagined by Bernini or Rembrandt,
we're the song, we're the lot of them,
heroes and their troubadours.
We shoot iron arrows in the bronze age,
we orgy on inconsistencies,
we sup sedately on irregularities,
singing and sometimes croaking our way
out of Spartan mess halls,
out of the pride of containment,
and the nightmare of nationality.

Wound

Is it all because we changed the boat's name
this wound won't heal, this fiery zero
in which all that mattered disappears?
Is each life a watch, a vigil, an eve
before a new star beast appears?
Did we trespass willy-nilly or did we dare
a feat we were warned against,
as black sheep do because they can?
This is the wound of the bastard son, his device,
sinister, glistening, unassuageable.
We have eaten constellations for lunch,
burped new worlds, and we are tired of gravity,
wary of magnetite and argument.
Our long service on the rim of zero ends
in knowledge that we are what comes next,
a blast from which, from whom nothing recovers,
nothing but our souls, all because we rode each word
to its combustion, until there was nothing left to do,
nothing calling on hubris to decide.

Tableware

He goes to his pocket not for a handkerchief but a phone.
Brooklyn Bridge is falling down.
Ships are docking a hundred stories high
while he tells another lie, sends a selfie
to an unsuspecting boy, looks down from a great height
while Brooklyn Bridge is falling down imperceptibly.
Who, he asks, is God now?
Falling down indiscernibly except to Sally
gathering sea glass at its feet, sea glass
ground from the tableware of nations' wrecks.
Goes to his pocket for a red cellphone while a single tear
refracts the misery of light. A selfie
that will perhaps tomorrow night remind
the boy of the cocoxsnut mask that woke him
when he sleepwalked to the kitchen, woke him
from a dream of ice cream carts and shabtis.
Where is Hells Kitchen? The orcas won't touch it,
but the sharks frequent Irish pubs and wear green bowlers.
And of this great height, O you who are queasy
about improbabilities, it's not exactly Fort Lee,
but it's far, far above remorse, a lawful high.
Sailors don't care what's going on below
in the city's bowels or even their own bilges.

They don't care this guy's already as big as Paterson,
bigger than a micro-climate, and getting bigger
the more he fathoms Sally's role
in his contemplation of his own evil. Falling,
Brooklyn Bridge is falling down, moorings crumbling
in Chinatown and the crushing piety of Williamsburg,
ambitions tattering in the wind, falling
without foofaraw as she gathers sea glass
and the gentleman with his frugal tear celebrates
his disintegration and forgets the colors of remorse.
Sailors don't care that every tear's an estuary
between severed parts. They have urgent work to do
stuffing mattresses into hull breaches, shutting hatches
on the rush of fools, work to do
like each fraught bead in Sally's hand, each former plate
from a captain's table, each innocence loosening
its hold on the boy,
each evil relinquishing the man.

Creepiness

dark electronic music   group chattering   muffled voices
laughter   please do vodka tonic
—all these disparities rotting steps to punctuate a fall.

A gathering creepiness somewhat like dusk
and yet a falling away as if day had been an interruption,
a kind of timeshare in which we sicken and die.

We're all short of breath, intubated, spasmodic,
our vitals driven up by needles and dire consequences
if we don't take this drug or if we do.

God help us then, God so poorly understood
we think him a special effect,
not a code we live to crack or be baffled by.

Even with more literate captions
and parenthetical explanations,
even if the credits slowed,
we can hardly figure each other out,
but what the hell, nothing stays in focus
and our conflated memories
are after all a work of art.

Forsythia

The story ends before you think
no matter what the progress bar says,
coitus interrupted by advertising,
and all the credits rolling down,
they were put in place, long,
so long before you think
you might as well have been a cursor
poking the vulnerabilities
as children poke dead animals
with a stick. The story ends
in a gaudy crescendo
even though you meant it to call to mind
a dour church rotting in a chortle of forsythia.

Peony On My Breakfast Plate

I think I must be going now
so that the Taconics will be okay,
so that bullfrogs will come out from under tarpaulin
and hop to the pond, so that
all that I've assumed may now be subsumed
in that glad mirror over there, subsumed into
that collider of into's, that cunt of time,
so that swindlers retired in Boca Raton may rest
assured one less person's got their number,
going now, my lips pursed as if to kiss
someone not quite recognized but ready
for adventure on Montauk Highway.
We have all been waiting for the seas to rise,
and yet we wish the glaciers well.
I should be going now, I tried to say,
but syllables fought off words
and I kissed the half-remembered girl too hard.
Excuse me, I think I've overstayed,
but I couldn't say that either, and I could see
it was going to be a project simply to apologize,
and would it have mattered if I'd managed to articulate
my embarrassment? Would anybody have cared?

Would it have made the slightest difference
if I had been understood, and does it matter now
t if I had been understood, and does it matter now
the Taconics are breathing better
that I understand this was never going to be
anything so felicitous as a shoe that fit
or a peony on my breakfast plate?
Where should I be going now? If I knew
why would I have loitered in a doorway
whose threshold rotted out,
at the foot of stairs kudzu climbs?
I wasn't meant to hang on doorknobs,
I wasn't born a skeleton key, and when I could speak,
when I'd learned the language, all I said was let me be.
I came owing rent, eviction notice in hand,
I go a sob of grief, a gasp, aghast to have stayed as long as this.

While We Sleep

water dripping   steps creaking
only a sob in the chest sounds like God
eaves groaning   rain splattering
divinity was too hard for us
knobs turning   pots clattering
so we chose to make our own gods
and hold them responsible for our cravenness
roses exhale rocks turn up   thunder
we are our own lightning bent
on showing creatures of the dusk
but we are their projections
having not even the decency
to hold hands before dawn
seams bursting   seas rising   cities heaving
life is what we deny   lies are drugs
truths come out to play while we sleep

To be still alive but only half yourself,
that's enough ignorance to start again

Who, for starters, was yourself,
and is oneself a trick of grammar
or something else again?

You hardly knew how to be alive.
Does one know any better?
hammer clangs   door bangs   neurons fry
And if your red blood cells now consent
to lug enough oxygen to your heart
you might grasp between gaps
this half life in half light
was at best a kind of rest in a sodden barn,
a vigil while you waited for this friend
stage managers call the end.

Fire Island

I

Now I set the yellow suitcase down.
Its latches startle bluebirds in their fencepost knots,
set marigolds to murmuring.
My life's underthings clamor for the light.
Their scents dizzy me.
I strew them on a row of burning leaves
and look up over the bay.
I think I'll stroll to Fire Island
now I feel this whorl of ancient light
surrendering its fancy.
I might even fly if I can pull myself away
from all this honey.

II

It's half past heaven, I'm running out of blood.
Never put much stock in vulgar notions of paradise.
I'm quantum physics' baby, leukemia's my rocket fuel.
Heaven? Don't worry about it,
I've visited it before, it's a waypoint on a great seesaw,
a brothel, a suburban heap, a sin, a sanctuary,
a pretentious din,
at best a museum to wander in.
I'm going to a wedding of particles,
going to be someone else, something else,
answering a summons to a reunion
the nostalgia in my bones struggles with,
that part of me that's always known
every second's half past heaven.

III

Ask me, ask me, Who the hell are you?
I'm everyone, all of them, all of you,
muon, gluon, axion, I aspire
to be anonymous. I send you flowers. You call me a liar.
So are you. We are God's particularities.
God's made of glee.
God is code.
This is not an ode.

IV

A choir of familiars flies to the lofts of my mind to sing
of what we'd made of each other and become
and as I I fall before the altar of the bay
a north wind combs my being
and lifts me out to the inlet
where the ocean waits.

Djelloul Marbrook

Djelloul Marbrook was born in 1934 in Algiers, Algeria, to parents Juanita Guccione (née Rice) and Ben Aissa ben Mabrouk. Marbook's father was Algerian and he moved with only his mother to New York City when he was a young child. He was raised by his extended family, primarily by his grandmother and aunts. Marbook grew up in Brooklyn, West Islip, and Manhattan. He attended Dwight Preparatory School, and Columbia University.

Marbook worked as a soda jerk, newspaper vendor, messenger, theater and nightclub concessionaire, and served in the United States Navy and as a Merchant Marine before beginning his newspaper career. Marbrook learned photography in the United States Navy and became a reporter-photographer. Marbrook was married to Wanda Ratliff from 1955 to 1963, which ended in divorce. He was married to Marilyn Hackett Marbrook, who passed away in 2022.

He was a reporter for *The Providence Journal* and an editor for the *Elmira Star-Gazette*, *The Baltimore Sun*, *Winston-Salem Journal* and *Sentinel*, *The Washington Star*, and *Media News* newspapers in northeast Ohio, and Passaic and Paterson, New Jersey. His poems, essays, and short stories are widely published in journals.

Djelloul Marbrook passed away on Saturday the 23rd of November, 2024.

His last two works were poetry and a memoir, this edition being his last collection of poems. His illustrated memoir is forthcoming in the Spring of 2026.

Whuddya See, Kid?
his new, illustrated memoir
is forthcoming Spring of 2026
by PIERIAN SPRINGS PRESS

Also by Djelloul Marbrook

- Marbrook, Djelloul (2008). *Far from Algiers: Poems.* Issue 14 of *Wick Poetry Serie*s. Ohio: Kent State University Press ISBN 9780873389877 Winner of the **2007 Stan and Tom Wick Poetry Prize**, and the **2010 International Book Award in Poetry**, explores the poet's feelings of not belonging to family or country.
- Marbrook, Djelloul (2010). *Brushstrokes and Glances: Poems.* Maine: Deerbrook Editions. ISBN 9780982810019.
- Marbrook, Djelloul (2012). *Saraceno.* Bliss Plot Press. ISBN 978-0-9718908-8-6.
- Brash Ice (2014, Leaky Boot Press)
- *Mean Bastards Making Nice* (2014, Leaky Book Press)
- *Riding Thermals to Winter Grounds* (2017, Leaky Boot Press)
- *A Warding Circle: New York stories* (2017, Leaky Boot Press)
- *Air Tea with Dolores* (2017, Leaky Boot Press)
- *Making Room: Baltimore stories* (2017, Leaky Boot Press)
- *Nothing True Has a Name* (2017, Leaky Boot Press)
- *Even Now the Embers* (2017, Leaky Boot Press)
- *Other Risks Include* (2017, Leaky Boot Press)
- *The Seas Are Dolphin's Tears*, (2018 Leaky Boot Press)
- *Light Piercing Water* trilogy (2018, Leaky Boot Press)
  - Book 1, *Guest Boy*
  - Book 2, *Crowds of One*
  - Book 3, *The Gold Factory*
- *Songs in the O of Not* (2019, Leaky Boot Press)
- *The Loneliness of Shape* (2019, Leaky Boot Press)
- *Suffer the Children: Sailing Her Navel* (poems) & Ludilon (novella) (2019, Leaky Boot Press)
- *Lying Like Presidents, New & Selected Poems*, 2001–2019 (2020, Leaky Boot Press)